HEAR MY CRY

Poetry and Prose

Elaine Catherine Christie

Published in the UK November 2019
By Restless Bones Publishing
6 Sherron Gardens
Birmingham
B12 9TG

ISBN: 9781999936105

To see a World in a Grain of Sand
And a Heaven in a Wild Flower
Hold Infinity in the palm of your hand
And Eternity in an hour

William Blake

PREFACE

You could say my journey towards this collection started in 2011, when I was looking for a higher purpose for my writing, a mission, if you will, when inspired by a white lion named Gandor, my writing turned to the white lions of Timbavati, then I came across Born Free Poet in Residence Richard Bonfield's 'Elegy of the South China Tiger,' after attending his launch of 'Animated Nature' I was so moved by his performance, I decided this would be my future path, not only to write about wildlife but to help in other ways too, so I became an Activator, Member and Fundraiser with Born Free Foundation.

I remember my Mother giving me the book 'Born Free' and being enthralled by it, the film remains a firm favourite of mine, another being 'Greyfriars Bobby' both are endearing films I enjoy watching over and over.

The charity has a unique and very special history. In 1964, husband and wife Bill Travers and Virginia McKenna travelled to Kenya to star in the classic wildlife film 'Born Free' based on the best-selling book by Joy Adamson. Released in 1966, the film told the true story of George and Joy Adamson's fight to return Elsa the lioness to the wild.

The Adamson's story was enjoyed by tens of millions around the globe, inspiring a generation and changing the world's attitude to lions forever. George Adamson MBE also known as Baba ya Simba ("Father of Lions" in Swahili) became a wildlife warden, and devoted himself to raising lions who could not look after themselves and training them to survive in the wild, including Christian whose previous owners where John Rendall and Antony Burke.

The lions that starred in the film 'Born Free' where also returned to the wild. Joy Adamson went on to rehabilitate a Cheetah named Pippa and Leopard named Penny.
Making the film profoundly affected Bill and Virginia, their close contact with lions sparked a lifelong commitment to wildlife, they realised wild animals belong in the wild, not incarcerated in captivity.
So, in 2011 I set out to help raise funds to rescue two lion brothers, Major and General from an army camp in Harar. With the help of Cathy Crossley, I hosted a poetry event to raise funds for Born Free Foundation, the lions were removed and are now in their nature reserve in Ethiopia. Since then I have hosted several poetry events for BFF, along with marches in Birmingham and helping at vegan festivals.
In 2013 I gathered some of my favourite voices in poetry, along with poets from the Animal Liberation Front, dog handler Janine Allen, and started to curate the 'Restless Bones' Anthology.
Josephine Wall's incredible fantasy artwork fitted my idea for the cover. Josephine, whom I am indebted to, graciously let us include a selection of her art to appear with the poems, edited by Jacqui Rowe and with the help of my friend Pat Clarke, 'Restless Bones' was launched at Akamba African Restaurant & Garden Centre on 21st August 2014, (the day after George Adamson's Anniversary) proceeds went to Born Free USA to help fight the fur trade.
'Hear My Cry' is a collection of poetry and prose on many facets of nature. From the imaginary tribeswomen of the Himalaya's, through the mysticism of Tulpa, to the valleys of Shaman, witness the creation of Kingfishers and Leopards, to the extinction of a species and the harsh realities of being an

animal activist. From Starlings to Lemurs, Borneo to Japan, with a dusting of magic it gives a voice to some animals and another universe to others.
A few of the images that inspired me can be found next to the verses, except for the horrors of certain cases, they are forever in my mind and perhaps should remain there.
These are letters of love, psalms for those we have lost, for nature concerns us all, their fight is our fight and it continues.

Elaine Catherine Christie
6 Sherron Gardens
Birmingham
B12 9TG

ACKNOWLEDGEMENTS

My thanks to the editors of the following magazines, anthologies and webzines in which some of these poems have appeared, in one form or another.

Poetry Rivals' collection 2012, Forever Words by Forward Poetry, The Women of the Pixie Chicks' Writers Group, An Eclectic Collage Volume 4: For the Love of Animals, Dial 174, Dawntreader, Silhoutte Press, Plum Tree Tavern Publishers, The Guardian, Warwick University Dodo, First Time, Born Free Supporters Poetry, World Wildlife Book, I am not a silent poet, Diverse Verse 2, The Friendship Collection Poetry Anthology, & Global Warning.

Thanks to Chris Manx Black Jaguar, Free Images, publicdomain.com, Pixabay Skeeze, GookingSword, Polyfish, Adobe stock photos, Sarah Lee Unsplash for all the photographs used to add depth to the poems.

Thank you to all the poets in 'Restless Bones' Anthology they continue to inspire me, especially Jacqui Rowe. To Josephine Wall for all her magical artwork within the book which made it extra special, also to Richard Bonfield, Virginia McKenna and the Born Free team in the UK & US, thank heaven for dedicated people like you, to all the charities working hard on behalf of wildlife, and the rangers who have lost their lives fighting to save endangered species.

For the many people whom have enriched my life and have helped me on my poetry journey, Julie Boden, Matt Nunn, Cathy Crossley, the Birmingham Stanza group, and especially to Neth Brown, Richard Archer and Jacqui Rowe they have been my sounding boards for this book.

CONTENTS

Hear My Cry

Listen with your eyes
to our wordless gaze,
set in asterisks from another universe.
A spiritual connection that says,
remember us as kin,
sawtooth wolves
sweeping the atoms of your mind.

Listen with your hands,
where our forepaws carved woodland circles
and our essence clings still warm,
remember us as kin,
sawtooth wolves
ghosting the foothills of your mind.

Breathe deeply with us
grassroot freedom, cedars and spruce,
our trail within their veins,
remember us as kin,
sawtooth wolves
pacing the shadows of your mind.

Let our hearts beat together,
your loneliness felt
in our broken-hearted ballads, on a dew claw moon.
Remember us as kin,
for we are calling you back, back to natures counsel.

Seeds

The tanzanite sweater that matched Dad's,
knitted lovingly by Mom.
Awkward legs feel heavy,
and move oddly in these red shoes.
The branded cattle path, sand-shifts
through peridot gem fields,
molten copper kissing infinite topaz.
Dad paused by drystone
lifted me castle high,
saying "Look at the harebells"
I sought rabbits in riffs of emerald,
Unaware of the five-pointed star.

I imagined under shade of adders tongue ferns,
hid mischievous bogarts and goblins.
Watched tufts of cotton grass sift and snag,
these were feathers of a broken angel
who carelessly slipped from the clouds.
Stripping stalks of downy grain,
satisfied at their crumbling
windblown dream-seeds, sprinkle from fingers.

Glorious scent of hay bales
dragon breath tamed and rolled.
Mother earth's amber eyes or
Rumpelstiltskin's wheels of gold.

The metal ting-tap of my shoes on railings
hesitating – I return to firmer footing,

sulphur sun tinselled a spectre in lame` threads,
alchemy's briary spell.
Dad showed me how to feed him,
picking meadowland,
rolling my palm out flat,
a tender touch -
wonderstruck by my first horse.

Naming Names

I am a mystic, a myth, a changeling.
I'm in the aroma of amethyst bells,
shadowed in the lowlands.
In the stave of swizzling starlings,
shimmering on twilight.
I am the coolness of icicle caverns,
in a darkened hideaway.
Or lost in the fury of flashing fireflies,
chasing loved ones.
In ethereal sun-slides
turning in kaleidoscope fashion,
through ancient Sequoia forests.
Or the passing puzzle
of the gawky giraffe,
to the pirouetting tail
   of a plummeting
     snow leopard,
       ghosted
         into atoms
           of a name.

My middle name Catherine was my Mother's name (however everyone called her Kathleen or Kath) I never use it, it's like empty space, like air, since writing this poem I have used my middle name.

How the Kingfisher Was Born (for Richard Bonfield)

I saw peeling feathers of Icarus, enflamed,
as curled cinders spiralled
like the last syllables of a star,
engulfed by viridian waves
tarping you in deaths spume.

Plectrums of tears were shed for you,
while in watery levadas
fizzmers of flashlight fish,
shone chakras of empyrean blue
and you were revived, reborn.

In Olympian pageantry
you speared the river Styx,
flared your fahrenheit armoury
lazuli and honeydew fisher king.

You are the desert and the oasis
you are sun, you are ocean
you are calmness, you are dance
you are dusk, you are dawn
the heavens and the earth,
you are forever.

Photographers Alan McFadyen & John Hannah taken by the River Tarff, Scotland.

Starlings

Wizardry unfolds here, in the bone spectre vastness.
Thundering chains of pterodactyls' rocket,
raw and rapturous in their wildness,
scythes that whiplash a doomed abyss.

Hypnotizing wing-prints on mazarine.
herculean leaves reading the inevitable eve.
A fevered dance of peacock psalteries
shivering and shimmying.

Soaring splinters and sparks, pulse to a farrier's beat,
the weightless whirr and swirl of a smithy's cauldron.
A crescendo of counters skateboard,
ripple, fuse, churn and concerto,
carving epitaphs on amethyst.
Magic incantations melt
as the sirens song,
descends into crickle - glass static.

The Return

I revisited once - just once
only the Sakura trees remembered me,
bowing as our fingers touched.

I moved into your embrace,
sat again, beneath Japanese gardens,
as Shinto blessings fell on sika deer,
gracefully treading prints of moon,
returning as their forebearers to Nara's temple.

Lanterns link each flowering tree to coastline,
where firefly squid are swept to shore
in the last dazzling moments of their lives.

My scarf wails around me
shivering as memories fade,
I turn away -
once - just once - I glance back.

Hollow

It's the permanent flux of polar nights,
ceaseless wind rises
stroking away footnotes of snowshoe hares,
hidden in a gauntlet of scrub.

It's the Snowy Owl
Grigori warrior on a knuckle dusted dune,
tomahawk raptor in a frozen papoose.

Watcher angel with gimlet eyes
her barcodes are counted sorrows,
scripted poems on parchment.

On haunting pipe sounds of the Chinook,
in the upward rush she extends her wings,
is swept softly by distance,
till just the wind remains.

Study of Trees

Countless chameleon faces
pause briefly
blend into surreal versions of oneself.
I see Wilfred Owen
coming over the hill
towards the Somme.
A crow
near a marble pillar
stares at a lycanthrope's head,
where a man and woman
are dead
in a hanging tree.
A black swan dissolves,
while a woman
plays hide and seek
with a lover.
The rabbit
watches Pegasus
in half gallop
bursting free from the banks.
A wendigo grimaces
from the varicose veins of an artist.

Based on the black chalk drawing opposite by Henri-Joseph Harpignies.

Tulpa

I am – the stardust sleepwalker
tip-toeing rainfalls of fireflies
surfing into auroras dolphin dancers
fading to ghostly geishas –
climbing again – into crest-falls of spirit fire
thought forms – sigils
grappling from grimoires
– now –
a smouldering tulpa –
I – was – once
almost real.

A tulpa is a Tibetan concept of a being or object which is created through spiritual or mental powers, "a mind-made body, magic formations generated by a powerful mind.

Fraying

Oracles of incense smother brushlands below,
where tribesmen have worn paths
that we have journeyed centuries before.
We are the spirits of the dead,
in the red dust sun, we have sat
cross-legged in arcane meditation.
We have tiptoed fraying air
to chase honey-dew cicadas.
Silver sashes ringing bell-tower trees,
our dark monocles highlight
our neon gaze, gargoyle-like,
stunned, as a blowpipe bleeds a threadbare future
into secret portholes of extinction.
We are the spirits of the dead,
we lie in the red dust sun in deep meditation.

Lemur means 'Spirits of the Dead'

Himalayan Ghost Queen

On moon shadowed monoliths
where weary clouds tumble
in a lens-turn
sepia pixels fuse with white jewelled sierras.
Smoke – is then form
the cosmos mirrored in a gaze
dappled beauty – the snow leopard.
Yakshini harlequin queen of starry spurs,
sky-walking red chiffon.
She is the guardian of the astral gates,
musket breath on dusky crags.

Nature-spirit of mountains and wilderness,
icescape artistry on champagne spires.
From her watchtower
spoors of travelling ibex haunt foothills below
her frame transfixed – then
with huge herding moccasins and winged tail,
she
melts
into
diamond
veneers
like
quicksilver,
scrolling
glittering
pillars

the
glacial
ghost
airbrushed –
into
myths
of
yesterday.

Yakshini are female mythical attendees of Kubera, Hindu God of wealth, imaginary people of the Himalayas.

Where Spirits Dance

Comets exhale dustcoats of
shooting rays on solar winds
heralding a golden timeslip,
where Norse Gods ride bloodstone storms
into dancing wells of stars,
touching far reaching tribes,
mirrored through portals,
where a magic glimpse of Aurora
goddess of the dawn, slip-steps.

The Sami still share the belief of their ancestors the lights emanate from the souls of the dead and must be treated with immense respect. The native American Cree tribe refer to them as the 'Dance of the Spirits.'

Story of the Wolf

Once revered as spirit healers and sentinel
by natives of the America's,
a community unified in blood
we shared mans fire in brotherhood.

You broke our bond we shied away
a nation of outlaws on the run,
fear has a hateful residue,
persecuted, we're now so few.

Legs snapped in razor tooth traps,
poisoned, shot, beaten and burned,
man had his victory over nature,
voices vanished into vapour.

In Utah you interfered with our DNA
crossed us with coyotes, dingos and dogs,
rabies erupted for your thoughtless fun,
again, we suffered, and it can't be undone.

Eradicated from England some 200 years,
Scotland, Ireland, worlds followed suit,
massacred for idle superstition
centuries passed without abolition.

No arctic paws on icebound shores,
Ethiopian reds disappeared too,
we timber wolves held our ground
endangered species law came around.

They relocated us to Yellowstone Park
we prospered into the Druid Pack,
again, man shot us, freedom staled
but our siblings live, to tell our tale.

Crossfire

I am in every war wheel and battle nest
in the mutilated misery, of shrapnel stung horses
or the vapours of broken elephants on land mines.
In the bloody bales of dolphins and sea lions,
bursting from ocean charges.
I am the expendable, weft into shrouds.

I'm in the soaking smog of a blistering plague,
in an orphan's shrill tears, as he pulls his mother's arm
raven eyed she gawps into an abyss.
I'm in the thread bare corpses, damson draperies
of death carved atrocities.

In the plumes of man's best friend,
loyalty traded for barking bombs.
In a mother's buckling, at a grey masked glyph
that was once her son.
In the hushed pendulum for the nameless lost,
I am the expendable, weft into shrouds,
I am indifference.

'Goodbye Old Man' by Fortunino Matania (1881 – 1963) picture is owned by Blue Cross.

Fabulous Fields

Such a sight I saw today,
where once these fields danced.

Two horses their hooves tied with twine
dumped, discarded, dead.
Have we forgotten their legacy of loyalty,
throughout history?
Pit ponies, died in falls from winches, or were forever
blinkered.
Coal cart horses, whipped and broken by their burden.
They have ploughed fields, pulled barges, wagons, drays,
trams, fire engines, ambulances and brewers carts.
Spirited sentients sold to the knackers yard to make soap.
Casualties lost in circuses, movies and tv,
others gored to death in bull fights.
Bartered, drugged and lashed for a bet,
shot, disposed of with spent slips.

War - a fools folly
the caltrop, truly the devils weed,
pierced and punctured
left you languishing in blooded muck.
Used as shields from bullets and bombs,
and the ultimate betrayal
of brutal barbarity -
they strung you up afterwards
human stomachs are your grave now.

In confessionals - men whisper
the number of wild mustang to be cleansed,
such a clean word -
but there's no godliness - in cull.

You're obsolete now -

such a sight I saw today,
where once these fields danced.

Dessert Lions, Absent With Out Leave (for Antony Owen)

I heard of an army camp in Harar,
where on concrete bunks
in a gunmetal boma
two captive cubs,
now haggard to restless years,
marching in the welting heat.

I contemplated their condition
as I was guided, three, last, miles, by roars.
The first thing you notice is their eyes,
shrunken sockets, hooded in bedrock,
black hair, barely tuft and dreadlocked.
Their ears had heard sounds of war,
their tall legs felt hostile tremors.
To cool down they panted
releasing sweat through their feet,
along with blood,
their pen lit up like slum neon.

They were the last of a kind.

In dusky lowlights
I gazed into night vision
six times more sensitive than my own,
and wonder,
if your mother long since dead
and the cautionary tale of men with guns,
will I be one of those memories
to jar your sleep?

Genocide Exists in Many Forms

In penumbral evenings, on rural steps,
a night rider lassos a sleeping spaniel
into a sack, gags him, slings him
over the back of his bike, already full,
disappears down the dirt road.

Taken to rows of Auschwitz cabins
crammed into overcrowded cages,
some suffocate, limbs break like china.
Unstable trucks journey to markets,
behind which, bunkers of blood stained walls
foretell their grim future.

Behind the meat stall on the floor is a large platter,
where a blowtorched spaniel crouches, its paws removed,
a child rests her hand on her lost pet
and lets out a piercing cry.

Tonight Mr Lee and his friends are going hunting,
three men wait in the shadows by the dirt road,
three men with blooded hands stagger home,
and a killer is taught, to let sleeping dogs lie.

Picking up the Pieces

A black sweater water soaked
looks like–congealed blood of a
faceless Rhino–earths stigmata.
Chip paper with remains of barbecued ribs
a Flamingo–some boys thought would be
fun to kick to death.
My gripper pulls a soggy carrier from the mud
leaving drag marks–of White Lions
hauled into cages for canned hunting.
A rubbish bag vomits on grass–
one grey glove–
the amputated paw of a Wolf
who struggled too hard.
Brown belt with large round buckle–
protrudes from a dancing Bear's nose.
A child's spotted slipper–
Cheetah Cubs killed for rich Arab feet.
Flattened coke cans–
crush videos from China
where women in stilettos pierce flesh
again and again and again.
Half full Dr Pepper bottle–
vinegar filled Victorian jars
of Tiger embryos–pickled
to make wine from their bones.
Earths gaping wounds,
rainfall can't cleanse.

Invisible Tribe

Through the spiralling red mists of a dust storm
a coppery-gold and black feline emerged.
Sleek, speckled with ethereal kisses,
an elegant shape-shifter with ninety nine inner eyes.
Freckle-faced, touched by a wizard's wand,
instilled with spiritual knowledge,
a unique instinct, and an illusionist's cape
so she can slip like a spirit between worlds.
She is the music of nature,
a phoenix reinventing herself
throughout time.

The Leopard is a legend
and when a legend dies,
dreams end.

When this poem was published, there were only 14 Amur Leopards left in the wild, in 2017 numbers have increased to 40.

Black Jaguar

At the bottom of the falls
on the shady swing of a banyan tree
ghosted by gas light
a Valkyrie sleeps in spirited fathoms.

Mountain Gorilla

Silver figurehead
primeval totem,
Virunga troglodyte
knuckle walking his highlands.

Giraffe

She's a strange arithmetic of angles
senegalia ossiconed sea horse,
eyes large as sunflowers
with parchment notes -
of saffron flames and lightning seams.

Unicorns of the Deep

Auroras fizz between stars
as two narwhals dive five thousand feet,
through a dazzling firework gallery.
Flashing photophores of octopus limbs,
shrimp spewing blue mists from its antenna,
marine worms erupt in showers of yellow sparks
as they unload their eggs,
luminous green eyed fish, gaze upward from grass cities,
and superorganisms with red lures on tips of tentacles.
As the unicorns exchange maps,
through millions of nerve endings,
sea-sparkle time-alters them
into ephemeral holograms.

The name "Narwhal"' comes from the Old Norse word nar which means "Corpse" referring to the whales mottled grey appearance which resembles that of drowned sailors.

Gifts

In the land of Timbavati, where white lions once trod,
who came from the stars, vessels of God.
The enlightenment bearers, a sacred life-form
targets for the trophy platform.

They were columns of light, bowing to no-one,
eyes humming-bird blue shone,
from huge wheat-grass crests,
to plush capes, curled upon their chests.

Swimming through scorched riffs,
love forged them from the land, a gift,
it is empty now, no sacred forms of white
just a haunting nimbus of gold, in a starless night.

A meteor struck the area of Timbavati in the 17th Century which resulted in the mutation of these creatures, locals thought it was a signal of enlightenment, new times, that the white lions were sent to earth as gifts by the Sun God. White Lions are only native to Timbavati. In 2014 only 13 original white lions remained, they are highly prized by poachers, many have been captured for canned hunting and inter breeding them has contaminated their gene pool.

Last of a Species

Reset your compass, burn all the maps,
leylines are broken, geysers are capped,
spillways of moon blur into sea,
it's last call for wildwood trees.

Mop up the veldt where blood is spilled,
the last rhino has been killed,
mourn the boneyards where horns were weighed,
bury the gold mines they've ceased to trade.

The Tigers Tale in Two Parts *(for Machli and Broken Tail)*

I came finally to the extreme forest
to see the secluded Empress of fire.
Her copper contours cooled beneath the surf,
as she weaved and waded, among river reeds
emerging on sweeping sands a fluid masterpiece,
an impressive frame with amber orbs that flashed.

A superlative image, mirrored in the sovereign's son,
who flared through quaking foliage,
a beltane sheeted script.
Avidly they feasted on fresh fish
lazily dozing after their fill,
their burnished honey robes, flattered by the sun.

II
"Mother, who are these titans that torment our terrain?"
The Empress sighed some wordless sorrow, then said
"Before the ark, before time began
we ruled every corner, before the titan.
Many have dropped like rag dolls in crimson seas,
they stripped our hides for ghoulish commodities.

I see no gilded faces in forests of green,
it is like our race have never been.
There are no granite headstones, to remember our dead,
no tears, or loving words, nor prayers be said.

So live fast my son, be all that you can be,
death waits, in the date-less night, unforgivingly.

But there will be a reckoning, of our races wronged,
and returning, rule again, the land where we belong."

Aftermath

In the holocaust of suffering
inflicted on our fellow creatures,
when the last of a species is snuffed out,
leylines shift, comets fall,
sun's filaments darken, oceans flux,
a kinetic howling gnaws,
leaving residual tears in the cosmos.

I like to think when they die,
they leap into a wormhole of dazzling stardust,
beyond are bear, great auk, cape lion,
with rhino, tiger and red gazelle.
I find comfort,
their beauty and instinct remain intact,
awaiting a new alignment
a world without man.

Sweeter Swell of Sun *(for George Adamson)*

Kora's veldt gleams rose-gold and imperial green,
Baba ya Simba's essence can be glimpsed
on the ghostly zephyrs of sun,
tip-toeing into orange ethers and charred remains.

In the valley of kings, a deep boned call
wing-whispers through crowns,
fluorescent flecks flash
as they follow their comrade,
cruising through brimstone mists.
Cubs calypso, rope tails reeling
into deep silhouettes, black pulpits.

There's a sweeter swell of sun - seen
before evening sets
a hallowed beauty
when nirvana is clasped.

George Adamson was known as Baba ya Simba meaning Father of Lions. Kora, home to George and Tony Fitzjohn for almost 20 years, has been rebuilt and made into a national park, to serve as a memorial and tourist attraction. A bridge has been built between Meru National Park and Kora – a dream of George Adamson's.

Home Fires *(for Virginia McKenna)*

I've seen it - in your eyes
It burns -
sienna-gold as the Serengeti sunrise.
It's in the blood-beat of your ancestors
left in claw print glyphs.
It carries on the scent of splicing rainfall,
on the soaring feathers of freedom,
in a warrior's steel digits fraying air.
In the breath of buffalo bones long sleeping,
long before shamans dwelt in spirit worlds,
or the ghostly pounding of tribal spears,
amid tumbleweed and dust.
In hooves fading into twilight wind chimes
and sunsets of mulled wine,
this is your treasure -
the kindling of home.

The God Particle *(for George Adamson)*

Through the moons phase and dusting of stars
windswept in emerald and crimson auroras
a polar bear ripples, in a disco inferno.
The glacier shape-shifter morphs, airborne
into a Neolithic shaman, in buffalo robes
riding a silver sled.

Creatures from every core, gazed upward
as the shaman in some mystic moment,
magnetically swept them skywards,
transmuting them
into glittering atoms on gossamer threads,
adrift the silver sled.

Lightening burst somber veils, echoing in lava pools
as the shaman sailed ahead, unfazed.
Humans agape, stared,
as they too were changed,
into cosmic ribbons
spiralling the sled.

On reaching the Himalayas white crowned peaks
the shaman released the atoms,
an avalanche of animals circled the summit,
then he freed the cosmic ribbons,
they too returned to human form.
Light trickled the roof of the world
from fuse to flame and beyond Olympic pageantry,
a glorious white lion

appeared in a nimbus of gold,
his glimmering mane, animated,
recoiled, curled, and swayed.
He roared to the animals
“I have seen your suffering at the hands of man
your day of reckoning has come"
then he roared to mankind,
“You must return to lessons of old."
A vista of snow circled the humans
instantly, they were reformed into animals,
another swirl,
the animals turned into humans.
The white lion roared again
"Each of you must know the others path,
correct all ills, time will then be reset
and everything will be as it should."
then the shaman melted with the lion
disappearing in a haze of gold- dust.

Cradle to Grave

In infancy they hung from mobiles above our cots,
from the arms of teddy bears to
puppets, cartoons, and sing-a-longs,
early books, rhymes and stories.
From nursery wallpaper –
to our gardens, farms and parks.
On birthday cakes, paper plates, cups,
spoons, feeding bowls and motifs on clothes.
Day trips, nature centers, zoos, to our first pets.
From TV, cinema, paintings, poetry, photography,
transfers, stickers, pens, pencils, erasers, sharpeners,
lunch boxes, mugs, glasses, toothbrushes.
To paper weights, door stops, cards, games,
scarves, socks, slippers and onesies.
Sculptures, statuettes, ornaments and carvings.
They are found on emblems, logos, shields and badges,
tattoos, jewellery, tapestries, needlework and buttons.
Curtains, cushions, pillows, blankets and rugs.

Animals are all around us,
seeping into every part of our lives
– so treasure them.

Artist Neth Brown

Neth Brown has been drawing and sketching from an early age, she studied Creative Writing, Journalism and Drama at Wolverhampton University. Her art takes on contemporary issues with hyper-realism and uses a variety of mediums, she has also experimented with photography and documentaries.

Neth designed the wolf picture for the cover and it appears in full next to the title poem 'Hear my Cry' she also sketched the shaman on page 49.

Neth is also a published poet, her work has appeared in anthologies and she performs in Walsall and around the West Midlands.

The Poet

Elaine Catherine Christie hails from the West Midlands and has studied Animal Care, Creative Writing and has a Diploma in Editing and Publishing. In 2011 she became an activator, member and fundraiser with Born Free Foundation, taking an active role in events and hosting poetry evenings to raise funds for the charity. In 2014 she curated and published the poetry anthology 'Restless Bones' all funds went to Born Free Foundation, to help in the fight against the fur trade.

This is Elaine's first collection, her poetry has previously appeared in Warwick University's Dodo, Trust Talk, First Time, Dial 174, Poetry Rivals, Forward Poetry, Dawntreader, Plum Tree Tavern Publishing, Pixie Chicks' Writing Group Volume 4: For the Love of Animals, Silhouette Press, The Guardian, I am not a silent poet, BFF Supporters Poetry, Diverse Verse 2, The Friendship Collection 'Childrens Collection' & Poetry Anthology 'Global Warning'. Elaine has currently taken over the helm from Jacqui Rowe at 'Poetry Bites' which she runs with co-host Matt Nunn.

Born Free Foundation
Broadlands Business Campus, Langhurstwood Road
Horsham, West Sussex,
RH12 4QP
(Charity Number: 1070906).

Born Free USA President: Will Travers
Born Free USA
P.O. Box 32160
Washington, DC 20007

Born Free USA's History

Animal Protection Institute (API) was founded in 1968: one of just a handful of national humane organizations at the time. Expanding throughout the years, API made significant contributions for animals for four decades.

Meanwhile, in 1984, Born Free Foundation was initiated in England by Bill Travers and Virginia McKenna, the stars of the legendary film Born Free, along with their son, Will. Born Free Foundation has since grown to become an international force in wildlife conservation and animal protection.

On January 1, 2000, API merged with the Texas Snow Monkey Sanctuary to form what is now known as the Born Free USA Primate Sanctuary Located in Dilley, Texas, the sanctuary provides a truly free-range environment for more than 600 rescued primates.

Born Free Foundation—Born Free USA—was established in the United States in 2002, with headquarters in Washington, D.C. In 2007, Born Free USA and API united under the Born Free USA name, combining forces for animals and to work to Keep Wildlife in the Wild around the world.

Jill Robinson MBE founded Animals Asia in 1998 – five years after an encounter with a caged bear on a farm in southern China changed her life forever. Learning that bear bile could be replaced by herbs, she vowed to put an end to bear bile farming. Since then, Animals Asia has rescued 400 bears in China and Vietnam. Jill is a Council Member of the World Federation of Chinese Medicine Societies (WFCMS) Herbal Committee and shares her home in Hong Kong with her three dogs and five cats.

Animals Asia is a registered charity with bear sanctuaries in China and Vietnam, headquarters in Hong Kong, and offices in Australia, China, Germany, Italy, the UK, USA and Vietnam.
Animals Asia Foundation is a company limited by guarantee registered in England and Wales (company number 4185603) and a registered charity (number 1086903).

Registered in England,
Charity Number : 209015.

Around the world as many as 200 million animals transport goods to markets, children to schools and water and supplies to remote communities. This essential but forgotten workforce of donkeys, horses, mules, camels and elephants supports livelihoods of over 600 million people worldwide - yet only a small fraction will ever gain desperately needed access to veterinary care. When working animals are sick, injured or in pain, there is no rest. Their hard lives are often short and filled with pain.

Soi Dog Foundation, 167/9 Moo 4,
Soi Mai Khao 10, Tambon Mai Khao,
Amphur Thalang, Phuket 83110,
Thailand.
Registration number: CHE-393.768.679

Soi Dog Foundation (Soi Dog) was established in 2003 in Phuket, Thailand, to help the street dogs and cats who had no-one else to care for them. Over 50,000 strays roamed the island, with the numbers growing alarmingly due to a lack of sterilization (spay/neuter) programmes to control the population. Soi Dog was created to provide a humane and sustainable solution to managing the stray population and to address their medical needs. Funding then, as it is now, came entirely from individuals who shared, and continue to share, the vision of our founders.

Environmental Investigation Agency Trust
62-63 Upper Street
London
N1 0NY
Registered Charity Number: 1145359
Our undercover investigations expose transnational wildlife crime, with a focus on elephants and tigers, and forest crimes such as illegal logging and deforestation for cash crops like palm oil. We work to safeguard global marine ecosystems by addressing the threats posed by plastic pollution, bycatch and commercial exploitation of whales, dolphins and porpoises. Finally, we reduce the impact of climate change by campaigning to eliminate powerful refrigerant greenhouse gases, exposing related illicit trade and improving energy efficiency in the cooling sector.

www.ingramcontent.com/pod-product-compliance
Lightning Source LLC
Chambersburg PA
CBHW042308080726
47818CB00035BA/371

* 9 7 8 1 9 9 9 9 3 6 1 0 5 *